kaleidoscope
poems in bloom

BY KAREN YELENA OLSEN
WATERCOLOR IMAGES BY JOAN ELKINS

Book composed in Quadraat
Book Design assisted by Virginia Woodruff
An audio version of this book is available, including musical interludes.

Published by Artpacks
Rochester, Minnesota 507/273/2529

first edition, 500 trade copies

ISBN: 978-0-9834637-3-3

My warmest thanks

to Joan, my inspired partner
in this poetic endeavor

also to Jay Jost,
for his peerless work
photographing Joan's artwork

to my mentors and fellow poets
for their sage advice and
encouragement, notably

Annalee Curran
Martin Hayden
Jim Lenfestey
Mary Olsen
Joseph Powell
Martie Shull
Natalie Ventura

to Virginia Woodruff, whose
artistry so enhanced the design
of these pages

to my beloved far-flung family
and to my friends here in Greece
and around the world, who are
always there for me.

for Dori, once again

CONTENTS

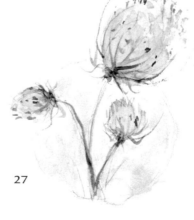

Autumn

About the Author and Artist

A Word of Welcome from Karen

As I discovered long ago in the Minnesota of my youth and confirmed in later travels, my days start best if I step outside, set off on a walk (around a lake or around the block), and look – truly look – at the world around me. All seasons, all landscapes offer their charms – a window box spilling bright colors onto a city street, a corn stalk sending its shadow over new snow, the pattern of lichen on a desert rock. And for many years now, I have found daily delight in my garden and especially in the fields surrounding my little village on the Greek island of Crete.

We set off in the morning, my dog and I. She is eager to investigate the scents left overnight by rabbit or mouse or marten, while I look forward to the pleasures of birdsong and the ever-changing pageant of wildflowers. Not a hike nor even a power walk, ours is a leisurely stroll, a half-hour loop along the paths nearest our small stone house, a few hundred yards at most. But there is so much to see, to look for!

As early as January here, even December, the arrival of spring inspires a swelling parade of blooms. It starts with the tiny pink and purple anemones, followed by the shy orchids in their bewildering array of shapes and colors. Later come the indigo irises, the sober gray asphodels, the bright pink glads. And finally, in a burst of gold, white and scarlet, the daisies and the poppies flood the fields.

The dry heat of the Greek summer sears the landscape, erasing this exuberance of color. The paths I walk now are dusty, with nature's palette reduced to muted shades of ochre, sepia, terracotta, olive drab, stone gray. But still my eyes delight in the faint lavender traces left by thyme and sage, in the stark architecture of roadside nettles, in the elegant limbs of the olive trees. At the same time, I am often tempted into reveries of the rich green fields and blue lakes of my childhood.

When the first rainfall of autumn breaks the long months of drought, the parched earth sprouts vibrant new growth. Dust-laden leaves regain their shine, ripening oranges and lemons glow on their branches, clover soon clothes the fields. And as fall elides into our brief winter, the tiny cyclamen pokes up through the rocks, beginning a new cycle of blooms.

In these poems and watercolor paintings, Joan and I invite you to walk along with us as we share our visions of this flowering world, in hopes that they may resonate with your own journeys into nature.

SPRING

SOLSTICE IN MY CRETAN VILLAGE

How the earth greens now!
On each hill and plain
shoots of grass spring forth wildly
to greet the new year

Once again I reel in shock
as at a gift arrived too soon

Bred in far northern climes
I carry still their grim ancestral memories

Those autumns so sad –
shadows lengthening
over fields desolate of corn

And winter –
that suicidal time of ice!

No wonder then I long misread
the setting of the Christmas scene

that homely birth
no less a miracle for being set
not in wintry black and white

but in such green as here
amid anemones purple and pink
in this due season of the lambs

SNAPDRAGON DREAMS

Black grains hide within shriveled husks
She taps them, rustling
from her wrinkled hand into my cupped palm
promising – next summer –
a rose-pink cloud of blooms

ALMOND BLOSSOMS

Following the storm
the tree is stripped
Rosy snowdrops carpet the path

Close to the Ground

Hyacinth amid the clover's green
Persian brocade
of lapis lazuli and jade

Gossamer Threads

A myriad tiny spider webs
weave among the periwinkle leaves
each cupping a single dewdrop
in its silvery gauze

WILD ORCHIDS

Country cousins
to those high-priced Asian beauties
you lack their pearly skin
their languid elegance

No thief will seek you out
to steal you from my field

Yet how I prize your inch-high pride!

Rising from the grass
each tiny petal flares
mauve opening to pink
lemon unfolding to cream

Eros glistens
in your dew-drenched lips
and whispers in your name –

Ophrys cretica orchidaceae

ELEGY FOR THE ORCHIDS

They have come and gone
leaving no trace
not a single frilly petal
in ivory or yellow or speckled pink
not one succulent lobe
opening to blackest indigo

Each has but a week to bloom
Away a month, I've missed them all –
save one

Hiding below the old-gold nuggets of Jerusalem sage
a miniature *orchis papilionacea*
its deep magenta shading to mauve
waves its tiny butterfly wings

TREES TOO

like the flowers
flaunt their seasons

First came
the lonely almond
brave in winter white

Then shone the rosy edge
of carob leaves unfolding

And now the sprays
of long-needled pine
are all festooned
with clustering cones-to-be
amber candles arching out
from every bough

That other evergreen
the subtle olive
glistens in spring rain

Nestled among its silvery shoots
each pale bud
as yet a small clenched fist
will open soon
to a brief and brilliant white

QUEEN ANNE'S LACE

Delicate disk of interlocking blossoms
each the immaculate white of Cretan lace
woven by Ariadne, crown for the bride

At the circle's center a radiant blush
spreads from a single blood-red bloom
hinting of royal passion and pain

EXTRAVAGANZA

This is the year of my orchid's triumph. Perhaps in Bangkok, its birthplace, my creamy-white beauty would elicit no notice. I saw so many show-off orchids there, often dangling carelessly from trees. Ah, but here, alone on my sunny kitchen window sill, it is spectacular!

This morning, as yet another blossom fans out like a butterfly, it joins the current chorus line of 27 exquisite flowers – with three more still in the wings, waiting to step forth from their pendulous green buds.

Each bloom is a study in sensuality, the five waxy petals surrounding a blush-pink cup, from whose lip two lascivious tongues curve out, then up and back toward its golden-stamened center. Together, cascading down the branching stem, the blossoms form a bouquet of fecundity. How very female these orchids! (despite the coy masculine origins of their name).

There is a lesson here too – about patience perhaps? I rewind to last spring, to the slow finale of the previous bloom. I watch the petals fall one by one, the stalk slowly shrivel, turn brown, break off. And then – for how many months? – the glossy leaves hover over my sink while I wash dishes, sip coffee, chop onions.

Austere through summer's drought, the orchid lives like some Asian saint, each Sunday accepting a mere spoonful of sustenance, the water barely wetting its roots. Above those shrunken limbs (twisted, tangled, bound within the pot), the leaves are a study in stillness, unmoved by the open window's breeze, calm amid the kitchen's clutter.

On the stone sill the sunlight shifts toward the shortening days of September. Then one fall morning I glance up, and my hand abandons its soapy sponge. I reach out toward a new tendril, a thin green finger curling up from the tuberous roots. Deliberate, purposeful, it takes its own sweet time – weeks to emerge from the canopy of leaves, more weeks to trace its graceful arc, spiraling up and out to new heights. At Christmastime the first knobbly buds appear. All through January, then February, they grow imperceptibly. And only now, with Easter again approaching, have those buds opened to their full glory. I am awed.

A Portrait

This April morning
the orchid bough bows down
under the weight of a dozen blooms

As the morning sun streams in
each blossom, backlit
reveals the secret of its form

The five white petals
translucent now
fan out around an inner three

Washed in pale yellow, pale green
their cores are etched with delicate
red stripes, thread-thin

These pastel frills curl round
the blossom's tight striated heart
suspended deep within

Down the heavy arc of the stem
only one green bud remains opaque
soon to unfurl its own snowy bloom

THROUGH FIELDS OF ASPHODEL

Your clouds of roseate gray
now shroud the farthest fields
your stalks so tall and sober
amid the riotous greens
of spring

And I see again Achilles' shade
adrift in misty Hades
heartsick at his fate
who yet
hearing Ulysses
praise his noble son
strides off, shoulders squared
through fields like these
of asphodel

On Seeing the First Gladiola

Pink pennants of the glad
flutter above the green-gold rye
flutes to herald the May

Jacaranda Tree in Bloom

A sudden spring gust
shakes the feathery boughs
lavender blizzard

Reweaving

Over and over
Spring – that fickle artisan –
reweaves her tapestry

Discarding April's
emerald and blue
her restless fingers
seize a skein
of paler green
entwining yarns
of gold and lacey white

And scattered over every field
she ties tassels of poppies
a scarlet fringe
for May's brocade

FENNEL GIANTS

High as my head the yellow wands
exult in the rising sap of Spring
How these hydra-headed stalks amaze!

Vanishing Act

A thousand irises welcome the sun
paint the green field blue
Come cloud, as sudden gone

Spring Alchemy

Last week
tramping through still fields
I came upon a vision

Amid familiar grays
of mist and sage
a malachite mirage
a pool impossibly Irish green
a jewel of liquid jade
set in the dry plateau

Today I speed my step
eager to repeat the scene

But no

The emerald field
has grown a thatch
blonde as my own
its flaxen fronds
rippling in the breeze

Gilded by the sun's first rays
green has turned to gold

LIFTING THE VEIL

Today
– at last –
my irises begin to bloom

All week
these tightly corseted buds
have risen
swaying on regal stems
each bound blossom
an iridescent indigo

And now
their leisurely unfurling
reveals pale lilac petticoats
scalloped and frilled
a Victorian lady's bloomers
silken déshabille

KALEIDOSCOPE

First the riotous colors of carnival
pinks and purples of anemones
porphyry glories of orchids
hiding among the rocks

Then a sudden shift to Lenten shades –
white carpets of Persian buttercup and camomile
snowy fringe of Queen Anne's lace

Sober gray stalks of asphodel
faint blush of tulips
pale mauve of blossoming sage
even paler green of olive bud

But long before the Easter feast
another spin of spring's kaleidoscope
brings banners of rosy gladiola

Forests of lime-green fennel
blue spikes of iris, gold of sorrel and broom
whole fields incarnadine with poppies
aflame in yellow daisies

My morning walk now sheer delirium

Naming

"Is that a cistus? Or maybe a rockrose bush?"
I've no answer to such questions

What I see –
a low shrub of sticky leaves, dotted with blooms
each flower hot pink
its five untidy petals circling a honey-gold core

A gypsy girl sways by in her gaudy flounced skirt
bare heels slapping the ground

This wise child asks nothing
sweeps past the shrub
strolls laughing back into the stony field
forever unnamed

Behind her the papery mauve petals
swirl and scatter in anonymous dust

SUMMER

Roadside Grasses

Last week their feathery green fronds
waved and fluttered in the mildest breeze

Today, unmoved by gusts and bluster,
these same stalks hang low

Their flaxen heads, swollen with seed,
bend humbly to the earth below

Pinwheels

Blue cornflowers hug the stones
their periwinkle whorls spinning across
the rocky floor of the field

Rite of Passage

Green to brown, a hillside suicide
overnight the clover died
and summer's drought arrived

ONLY THE HERBS ENDURE

The Mayday wreath fades on the door
its poppy reds long fled
from these arid fields –
mere husks
in a rustle of dry grass

But the cool gray spears
of sage and lavender
the green
of piney rosemarie
of lemony verbena –
these still endure

And as the caper's bridal spray
ripples down the rocky scarp
each cleft in the stone below
thrusts up its clump
of pungent purple thyme

TO THE LAKE

In the still cool of dawn
a mourning dove
whistles its three-note spell
and suddenly restores
a summer's morning
forty years before

Breathing in the dew
of lilac and mown grass
I race my shiny red bike
past fields
where horses stand asleep

Plump legs pumping, I pant
up and up the last rise

then push off
tires thrumming
for a wild spin
down to the pine-dark lake

Padding out on the dock
I shiver in wet wool
curl my toes against the worn planks
then lean into that first dive
tasting its mossy depths

On the far shoreline
mirrored among willows
the sinuous wake of a lone canoe
and the call of a loon
whistling across the water

Solstice

Awake to mark this shortest of nights
adrift in the empty field
now bathed in moonlight
I pause
rest my hand on the hive –
by day bee-loud
a dangerous hum
now silent, shadowed
honey-sweet

Immersed in the summer's fullness
bowed to the searing months ahead
I yet feel tonight
earth's slow, inexorable shift
its tilt
toward September's
mellow, balanced days
and the moonless dark
of December

In July

this heady time of thyme
a thousand tiny blossoms
fragrant in the heat
cast a lavender veil
over the sunburned fields

From the olive trees above
the cicadas' restless
ceaseless buzz
numbs us to silence

THISTLES

Gone the frail orchids, iris, ferns
even the hardy daisies of May

now rise nettles, thistles, thorns –
tough denizens of drought

stiff plumes of paintbrush
sweep whole fields into a purple swirl

low and solitary sunbursts
glow gold beneath the olive tree

pale green buds blush
within their cages of spun wire

from the wickedest of spikes
sprout tiny trefoil leaves

Soon these too will shrivel
their green fade to gray

laying bare
an intricate geometry

abstract skeletons
of iron briar and spine

each barb set to snag
the bone-dry heat

of summer

QUIET DELIGHTS

Always
I have loved the silence of dawn
and its small sounds
heard only in solitude

A girl growing up in the north
I woke in summer
to the who-are-you who-are-you
of the mourning doves
or the splash as a fish
broke the surface of the lake

In winter
my frosted window open
just a crack
I heard the muffled thud
of snow clumps
sliding off the branches
of the overburdened spruce
Burrowed in bed
I listened to the gritty scrape
of the neighbor's shovel
grating against his steps

Here in sultry August
I wake to the owl's lone hoot
cast out over the sleeping village

In the first light the breeze rises
lifting the branches of the olive
rustling its dusty leaves
welcome end to this still, hot night

SIROCCO

Through the black night
the wind comes howling
dread tongue-lash out of Libya
whipping across the sea
to sandblast our land

As shutters bang and slam
I race out into the loud dawn
bucking the gale
in hopes to latch the garden gate

Too late

On twisted hinges it yawns agape
I lean to heave it up
then let it fall

What's left to protect?

The avocado's gone
its green gloss curled to brown

Below the shredded citrus leaves
green lemons small as olives
litter the caked clay

My snow peas
sparse and shrunken as they were
now dangle from bare stalks

In all the parched field
only the natives survive –
leathery sage and lavender
clumps of thyme
huddled to the ground

Back in April
buoyed by the false hopes
and homesickness
of transient spring
I'd planted scores of catalog seeds
dreaming the fragrance of mint
and lemon grass and chives

Drunk on their names
I ordered coriopsis, caerulea
achillea debutante
moon vine

From bare roots I conjured
the northern tang of berries
red and blue

Eyeing me the villagers
so frugal of water
(of laughter, of love)
spared only a grim smile
for my extravagance

In turn I watched them plant
tomatoes, garlic, cucumbers
saw them prune their sturdy vines

Scorning their prosaic yield
I mourned as well their shrunken dreams
stunted by lives as hardscrabble
as their romances, their joys

Ah yes but even in May
my losses were high

Though coaxed and cosseted
into lime-green leaf
and fragile bloom
my exotic aliens soon shriveled
then died

Today
stunned by the whistling heat
I break off the final brittle cane
pull out the last dry root

My angry rake scratches across clods
rattles the leaves
raises devils of red dust

And only now
as the sun arcs
into a bleached denim sky
do I bend to the wind's bitter truth

AUTUMN

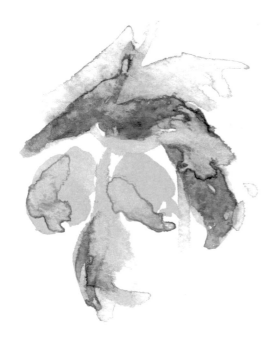

LEAVES

Here, Fall is no noun
worthy of the name –
just an exhaustion of summer
a wait for winter's rain
I plod, kick stones
grumbling

But now, under my toe
from some insignificant thistle
flares up a single rosy leaf

igniting that forgotten season
when
small schoolgirl
I shuffled in delighted rubber boots
though a deep rustle
of red and gold

In the dusk of Saturdays
I leaped
screeching with joy
into the soft mountain
of a whole day's raking

The crumbled leaves of oak
caught in my cuffs
in the pockets of my plaid shirt
colored the slant light
of Monday's lessons
(China in yellow chalk
its rivers pale green veins)

and all the musty ghosts of
wooden desks
India ink
cloakrooms
and lunchbox apples
rise
from this solitary leaf

AUTUMN PALETTE

Gazing out at this September dawn
I smile to find
my sere fields
so stylishly adorned

From weeds to trees
all sport the fashion season's latest hues –
sage green, burnt ochre, olive,
terracotta, charcoal, stone

And now the sun appears
ivoire, écru
a pale medallion, *faux bijou*
rising into a *cerulean* sky
blushing in
russet
then in *pearl*
now in *dusty rose*

SEA SQUILL

Autumn cousin of the asphodel
it rises high above the wind-swept field
a myriad tiny petals cling
– white on red –
to the waving stem

A lone feather quill
scribbling invisible script
upon the azure sky

In September

the apricot tree is ablaze in green and gold
each lingering leaf a flame
Will I taste again those succulent globes of June?

Rainbird

Winging over the parched land
spiraling above the desiccated trees
crowing loud to the dark clouds
massing in the west
she beckons the rain

And it comes! It comes!
those sweet, heavy drops
that pucker the dust
then patter
then pound
soaking into the earth
puddling into mud

As the clouds scud and billow on
other birds wake
to sing the greening of the land
but high and silent
in the scented air
the rainbird soars

On her wings
she lifts our hopes
in her wheeling flight
she heals our dreams

As the Storm Passes

the white morning sun silvers the olive trees
now gleaming against the blue-black sky
their leaves, rain-bright, quiver in the wind

Following the Rain

All night the black air rumbled
as invisible drops
spattered into our dreaming ears

Now in the rinsed-clean dawn
colors rush back
hues we had forgotten
all these long hot months of drought

Tree trunks
stripped of their drab uniform of dust
shine like obsidian
while leaves of olive and carob
needles of cypress, clustered spikes of pine
all flaunt their separate flags of green

Dashing through the brush
my dog, nostrils flaring
flushes an ecstasy of odors –
astringent eucalyptus
pungent sage
intoxication of thyme

The rocky hill above
so long bereft of bloom
seems barren still

But then
kicking aside a sodden twig
I glimpse a flicker of pink

Sudden as a mushroom
a cyclamen has arched
out of the fissured stone
holding aloft its inch-high
feathered headdress of hope

IN THE CITRUS GROVE

After the rain
the path a limpid pool
cloud mirror

Below still-dripping trees
the clover, emerald green
thick, wet-heavy
crushes under my galoshes

Above my head
the ripe globes hang
among the glistening
green-black leaves

Chinese lanterns
glowing orange
lemon yellow
blood red

PRUNING THE OLIVE TREE

Slowly, slowly I circle the tree
muttering the Cretan mantra
inverted umbrella, upturned cup

First random rapid snips
paring away the obvious excess —
scrawny shoots
wavering up from the roots
wayward twigs that point
inward
or sideways
or down
toward the clover-covered earth

All too soon I slacken pace
reluctant to lop
this vibrant bough
loathe to spoil
that hint of symmetry

Assailed by doubts
I falter   stop   step back

Then, drawn by the blue space glimpsed within
I kneel, part the bending branches
enter the still center

Embracing the worn trunk
I look out and up
following the tree's own thrust
and suddenly
its sap flows in my blood
its branching growth guides my hand

Saw and shears now easy in my grasp
we do our surgeon's work

When I stand back at last
it is the clean bones I see

The arching arms reach out
through bright new leaves
the tree's pure skeleton revealed
a cup containing the sky

Text Message

Climbing the hillside in the morning chill
I fumble, startled by the buzz

How r u? C u @ 10?

My fingers too stiff to punch the keys
my voice strangled by this tongueless text
I pocket the phone

And how to impart by *SMS*
the rosy flush of dawn
now warming this stony slope?

What symbol for that red hawk soaring?
for the rainbow caught in the trembling drop
pendant from that olive leaf?
for this anemone
tiny scrap of indigo silk
pushed up by last night's rain?

And what *emoji* for my heart
lifted by this wordless scene
yearning toward our rendezvous?

Im OK
Yes @ 10
xoxo

COLD SNAP

I step outside
my "Oh!" a white puff of sudden wonder

Setting off across the grass
now felted in frost
my boots rustle
through tangled threads
of silver lamé

Ice dusts the fuzzy leaves
of rockrose and sage
etches the spider's lace
and the roadside nettle's spikes
rimes the crystal petals of pink anemone

As I splash through the glass
of yesterday's puddle
its thin mirror shatters
into a spray of sequins
sparkling across the morning's misty chill

In an hour this glittering vision will fade
to a muddy rug of greens and grays

May it last a little while longer
that I might still linger
rapt in its shivery spell

The Author

Though Minnesota born, Karen Yelena Olsen has been living in Greece for many years, first in Athens, and for decades now on the island of Crete. She began writing poetry while maintaining a career teaching literature, mythology and composition to the adult students of the University of Maryland European Division. Several of her poems were published in Poetry Greece (2000), others in a 2012 chapbook, And Life to You: Elegies in a Foreign Land. An amateur pilot married to a professional aviator, she compiled and edited the anthology On the Wing: American Poems of Air and Space Flight (University of Iowa Press, 2005).

In the company of their beloved dog and a half-dozen free-range tortoises, Karen and Dori live in a small stone house nestled in a shepherding village high in the Cretan hills. The village is the focus of her current work-in-progress, a book of poetry and prose entitled Island Almanac: Seasons of a Life in Crete.

Karen has always been drawn to art and artists; both And Life to You and the Almanac are illustrated with line drawings by the talented Jerry Glover. But she knew that the wondrous shapes and hues of the flowering world inspiring Kaleidoscope demand the polychrome palette of watercolor. What a gift then to work with Joan, whose rich, flowing vision echoes and enriches the intent of these poems.

Contact: alonicrete@gmail.com

The Artist

Impassioned by the arts, Joan Elkins graduated from Lawrence University in Appleton, Wisconsin in 1967, with a BA degree in violin performance and a minor in art. She played professionally in Milwaukee, Wisconsin and Australia before returning to Rochester, Minnesota, where she continued her musical career and later worked for a retreat center and hospice.

Now semi-retired, Joan has relished the time to renew her passion for watercolor painting. Long inspired by Karen's poetry, she was delighted by the opportunity to collaborate with her lifelong friend in creating images for this book. She feels that the fluid nature of watercolor best reflects the vibrant and fleeting life of flowers that inspired Karen's poems. Fond of the suggestive nature of haiga, a visual form of haiku, Joan strives to evoke a similar feeling of immediacy and simplicity through her watercolor images.

Contact: joansnikle@gmail.com